ARE YOU
LIVING
THE
GOOD
LIFE?

Randy Alcorn

ARE YOU LIVING THE GOOD LIFE?

Tyndale House Publishers, Inc.
Carol Stream, Illinois

Visit Tyndale online at www.tyndale.com.

Visit Randy Alcorn's website at www.epm.org.

TYNDALE and Tyndale's quill logo are registered trademarks of Tyndale House Publishers, Inc.

Are You Living the Good Life?

Designed by Jacqueline L. Nuñez

The author is grateful for the helpful counsel of the literary agency, WTA Services LLC, Franklin, TN.

For information about special discounts for bulk purchases, please contact Tyndale House Publishers at csresponse@tyndale.com, or call 1-800-323-9400.

This book is adapted from *Giving Is the Good Life* © 2019 by Randy Alcorn.

ISBN 978-1-4964-4376-2

Printed in the United States of America

25	24	23	22	21	20	19
7	6	5	4	3	2	1

CONTENTS

YOUR INVITATION TO THE GOOD LIFE

Give away your life; you'll find life given back, but not merely given back—given back with bonus and blessing. Giving, not getting, is the way. Generosity begets generosity. LUKE 6:38, MSG

CHANCES ARE, you were drawn to this booklet because you want "the good life." Perhaps your life hasn't lived up to your expectations and hopes. And even if you're not quite sure how to define the good life, you know you'd like to experience it. After all, who wants to live "the bad life"?

Google "the good life" and you'll find advice from both secular and religious sources on how to achieve a life worth living. We're told, "Make lots of money, spend it on yourself, and you'll be happy. *Then* you'll be living the good life!"

That's a lie. Despite a long history of personal

experiences and studies indicating money doesn't—indeed, cannot—buy the good life, countless people make choices as if it does. Yes, we all need food, clothes, and shelter. But once our basic needs are met, money often stops helping us and starts hurting us.

In 2007, actor Owen Wilson slashed his wrists in an unsuccessful suicide attempt. *People* magazine's cover story about the "funny man who had it all" implied that his material abundance gave him every reason to live. Public shock over his actions unveiled the widespread belief that things like money, fame, cars, sex, a second home—the whole celebrity package—really do buy happiness. After all, wasn't Owen Wilson living the good life?[1]

In a subsequent issue of *People*, one letter to the editor insightfully asked, "If a red-hot career, traveling the globe, a Malibu mansion and million-dollar paychecks didn't prevent Owen's 'demons' from rearing their ugly heads before the August incident, why would they do the trick now?"[2]

The irony is inescapable: most of Owen Wilson's fans would have, in a heartbeat, exchanged their mundane, commonplace lives for that of their idol.

But the trade would have given them the life Wilson desperately wanted out of.

Throughout his ministry, Jesus told us that parting with money to help others actually brings us more joy than holding on to it for ourselves. Counterintuitive as it may seem, our greatest good, and the happiness that accompanies it, is found in giving, not receiving.

In other words, generosity *is* the good life.

Deep down, we all know we can spend every last cent on ourselves and still end up miserable. In fact, that lifestyle *guarantees* we end up miserable! What Jesus calls us to do is far more radical and satisfying: love others by giving away our money and time. That sounds like loss, not gain, right? Yet in God's economy, that's exactly how we expand and enhance our own lives.

I'm not suggesting that giving always comes easily or without sacrifice. I *am* saying that in God's providence, the payoff for living a generous life far outweighs—and outlasts—the sacrifice.

Jesus told his disciples that when they gave money away, their hearts would follow the treasures they were storing in Heaven (Matthew 6:19-21).

He also said that at the Resurrection, God would reward them for helping the needy (Luke 14:14).

The Bible shows that anything we put in God's hands is an investment in eternity. That doesn't just mean that our giving will bring us good someday in Heaven. It will also bring us good here and now—*while* it does good for others. That's why the good life is inseparable from generosity.

Sound too good to be true? Well, keep reading! Because, as you're about to discover, the truth about living the good life is far better than you could ever imagine. And because of Jesus, it's absolutely possible for you—regardless of your income—to experience it.

WHERE DOES THE GOOD LIFE BEGIN?

If anyone thirsts, let him come to me and drink. Whoever believes in me, as the Scripture has said, "Out of his heart will flow rivers of living water." JOHN 7:37-38

To UNDERSTAND WHAT constitutes the good life, we need to grasp where life comes from and where it's going.

God is the eternal source of life. He gave human beings "the breath of life" (Genesis 2:7), and he designed the first people to experience communion with himself, the living God. In the presence of Eden's tree of life (Genesis 2:9), he walked with Adam and Eve as they enjoyed a life-giving and delightful relationship that ended when they sinned

(Genesis 3:8). God warned them that if they ate of the fruit of one particular tree, this beautiful life would tragically end in death (Genesis 2:17).

They disobeyed. And while Adam and Eve's physical death came gradually, the end of their life-giving spiritual relationship with God was immediate.

Ever since, people have existed in a state of spiritual death: dying bodies, decaying relationships, and failed dreams. Death is the new normal. But that's not the end of the story. The Good News tells us Jesus' sacrifice conquered sin and death on our behalf.

God created the world through Jesus, bringing life and light to his creation (John 1:1-5). Jesus rose from the grave, ensuring the ultimate death of sin and the defeat of death itself. His resurrection gives us life (Romans 4:25). In fact, his resurrection is the basis for God moving us from death to life (1 Corinthians 15:17).

Jesus calls himself *life* in these four passages:

- the bread of life (John 6:48)
- the light of life (John 8:12)

- the resurrection and the life (John 11:25)
- the way, and the truth, and the life (John 14:6)

Jesus also said, "Truly, truly, I say to you, whoever hears my word and believes him who sent me has eternal life. He does not come into judgment, but has passed from death to life" (John 5:24).

John tells readers his Gospel was written "that you may believe that Jesus is the Messiah, the Son of God, and that by believing you may have life in his name" (John 20:31, NIV). Jesus said to the Father, "Now this is eternal life: that they know you, the only true God, and Jesus Christ, whom you have sent" (John 17:3, NIV).

Jesus is not just a signpost or a compass to life; he *is* life. He's not merely a map leading to water or an X that marks the spot where treasure is buried. Rather, he *is* the wellspring. He *is* the treasure.

The first step to finding life is clear: we need to place our lives in Jesus' hands. That's where eternal life—the ultimate good life—begins.

ONCE WE BECOME JESUS-FOLLOWERS, HOW DO WE EXPERIENCE ABUNDANT LIFE?

I have come that they may have life, and that they may have it more abundantly. JOHN 10:10, NKJV

ALIGNING OUR IDENTITY with Jesus' death and resurrection gives us power to live authentic, righteous, and beautiful lives, so that "just as Christ was raised from the dead by the glory of the Father, we too might walk in newness of life" (Romans 6:4). This is a vibrant life overflowing with God's grace—what 1 Timothy 6:19 calls "the life that is truly life" (NIV). In other words, it's *the good life*. And it's available to everyone who follows Jesus.

But though we've been granted eternal life, even many Christians don't fully experience the joy Jesus offers. Why? Scripture warns that Satan despises us and seeks to destroy us by robbing us of the good life God originally gave Adam and Eve—the life Christ came to restore to humanity. Satan convinces us that money and possessions are the source of abundant life.

Attempting to experience the abundant life Jesus spoke of while burying ourselves in material abundance isn't just difficult; it's impossible. While possessions may be neutral or even fun, it's too easy to end up trusting our stuff instead of our Savior and suffocating under the accumulation.

If abundant stuff equaled the abundant life, wealthy unbelievers wouldn't need Jesus. Materialism dresses up the corpse and puts makeup on it, but it's still dead. Jesus redirects us from death disguised as life to true abundant life. He says he came into the world to give us "a rich and satisfying life" (John 10:10, NLT) or "life to the full, till it overflows" (AMP).

The more we give in Christ's name, the more his life flows into us. And the more life flows into us, the more that life flows out to others. "Give, and it will be given to you," Jesus said. "A good measure, pressed down, shaken together and running over, will be poured into your lap" (Luke 6:38, NIV).

By giving generously of our money and possessions, we're able to open our hands to receive the abundant life God has for us.

WHAT'S THE BAD NEWS ABOUT MONEY?

Better a little with the fear of the LORD than great wealth with turmoil.   PROVERBS 15:16, NIV

IN TWO POWERFULLY descriptive verses, the apostle Paul concisely reveals this list of the perils of falling for Satan's deception by craving wealth:

Those who desire to be rich fall into temptation, into a snare, into many senseless and harmful desires that plunge people into ruin and destruction. For the love of money is a root of all kinds of evils. It is through this craving that some have wandered away from the faith and pierced themselves with many pangs.
1 TIMOTHY 6:9-10

The desire for riches is inseparable from "many senseless and harmful desires." These desires "plunge" many into ruin and destruction, because fools inevitably make choices that harm themselves and those around them. The Greek word rendered "plunge" in twenty-nine English versions is translated "drown" in seventeen others.

The life described here is the polar opposite of Jesus' promise of a "life in all its fullness" (John 10:10, NCV). Loving riches is not the good life. It's a deeply dysfunctional and spiritually impoverished life—one that both serious studies and casual observation confirm leads to moral decay, sexual sin, family breakdown, loss of faith in God, and ultimately death.

If we allow this passage to guide our thinking, we have to ask: What are the payoffs for stepping into a bear trap? What is the profit in drowning? What is the upside of ruin? What are the benefits of destruction?

No one in their right mind would desire grief, sorrow, pain, and agony. Nobody wants to pierce, wound, or impale themselves. Yet God says that's *exactly* what we do when we choose to center our lives on money and things.

Chuck Swindoll writes, "Money can buy medicine, but not health. Money can buy a house, but not a home. Money can buy companionship, but not friends. Money can buy entertainment, but not happiness. Money can buy food, but not an appetite. Money can buy a bed, but not sleep. Money can buy a crucifix, but not a Savior. Money can buy the good life, but not eternal life."[3]

In short, money's power is extremely limited, and consistently deceitful.

"Better a little with the fear of the Lord than great wealth with turmoil" (Proverbs 15:16, NIV). While the poor can have plenty of turmoil, great wealth is nearly inseparable from its own kind of turmoil. The fact that money-induced trouble takes us by surprise shows that we expect wealth to satisfy us when it has no power to do so.

That's why we should regularly ask ourselves, *What will be the consequence of this purchase? What would be the result if I gave or saved that money instead?* Sure, God intends for us to find pleasure in some wants along with our needs. But when we aren't careful, money-love traps us in a lifestyle that dishonors God and harms us and those we love.

IS MONEY REALLY EVIL?

The love of money is a root of all kinds of evils. It is through this craving that some have wandered away from the faith and pierced themselves with many pangs.   1 TIMOTHY 6:10

THOUGH IT'S COMMONLY MISQUOTED, 1 Timothy 6:10 does *not* say, "Money is the root of all evil." Rather, it states that "the *love* of money is a root of all evil."

Money itself is not inherently evil. What we *do* with money can be either good or bad. Money can be used to bribe a judge, buy cocaine, and fund terrorist acts.

Money can also purchase life-giving aid, feed a family, further the cause of justice, and fight oppression. Money can help build wells, finance housing, save children's lives, support churches, and fund Bible translations for unreached people groups.

If money were evil in and of itself, it could not be used to do such good!

Every time we do anything with money—for instance, spend it, save it, or give it—we get something in return. If we buy sex, we've used money for evil. If we buy food for children, we've used money for good.

We prove our love of money when we always hold it close or spend it on countless things we don't need. The wrongful pursuit of wealth destroys morality, marriages, families, business relationships, church relationships, and everything else, while robbing us of contentment and happiness. It results in spiritual ruin because money-love always displaces God-love.

Jesus said, "No one can serve two masters. . . . You cannot serve both God and money" (Matthew 6:24, NIV). We can use money to serve God. But it's impossible to serve both.

Even when we recognize the threat of money-love, it's difficult to avoid its grasp. Materialism is behind advertising, spending, credit, and debt. It drives entertainment, music, and sports, and some-times it even drives churches. The pursuit of wealth is so frequently hammered into our thinking that we would have to live in a cave to avoid its allure. Therefore we must chase something greater than our culture—God and his Word—in order to resist these temptations.

WHAT'S THE GOOD NEWS ABOUT MONEY?

No one can serve two masters. Either you will hate the one and love the other, or you will be devoted to the one and despise the other. You cannot serve both God and money. MATTHEW 6:24, NIV

AFTER WARNING AGAINST desiring to be rich in verses 9-10, in 1 Timothy 6:17-19 Paul gives commands that to some might seem restrictive, but to those who understand are utterly liberating:

Command those who are rich in this present world not to be arrogant nor to put their hope in wealth, which is so uncertain, but to put their hope in God, who richly provides us with everything for our enjoyment. Command them to do good, to be rich in good deeds, and to be generous and willing to share. In this

21

*way they will lay up treasure for themselves as a firm
foundation for the coming age, so that they may take
hold of the life that is truly life.* (NIV)

This passage recognizes that Christ-followers
with extra resources can please God, serve his pur-
poses, receive eternal rewards, and find true purpose
and fulfillment in this life. It's good news that we
can, despite the many biblical warnings about want-
ing to be rich, honor God by recognizing that everything belongs to him, by asking what he wants us to
do with it, and by giving generously. The outcome is
both future rewards and present contentment, purpose, and what Scripture calls "the life that is truly
life" (1 Timothy 6:19, NIV).

Alan and Katherine Barnhart have given away
more than $100 million from their company.
Furthermore, they have given the company itself to
God and his Kingdom. I mean this literally. Family
members can work there, earning normal salaries,
but neither the Barnharts nor their children or
grandchildren will ever own the company's financial assets. At a Celebration of Generosity event,[4] I
enjoyed hearing what their adult son Nathan, then

in his twenties, shared about growing up in their home.

"We were raised in a culture of generosity and contentment," he explained. Then he told an unforgettable story.

"When I was probably eleven or twelve . . . I went to my dad and said, 'Hey, Dad, I think we should get a Hummer.'"

"Nathan, that's a great idea," his father said. Then he surprised Nathan by saying, "What if we got *two* Hummers?"

After letting that sink in, Alan said, "I can do that for you. . . . In fact, I could buy you enough Hummers to fill up our driveway."

Nathan said, "We had a really long driveway . . . so I'm thinking, *This is too good to be true. Where's he going with this?*"

His dad then asked him, "What if we took that money and instead blessed . . . people who don't know where they're going to get their next meal or don't know where they're going to sleep at night? Nathan, there are thousands, millions of people around the world . . . who don't have access to the gospel. What if we used that money to bless them?"

Nathan's genuine response, from his heart, was, "That is a great idea!"[5]

The Barnharts' story demonstrates it's possible to use material wealth in a way that says no to temptations and builds God's Kingdom. It's possible to show our children and others that God doesn't entrust money to us just to increase our standard of living but to increase our standard of giving.

This family cheerfully lives out the commands of 1 Timothy 6:18, which says to "do good, to be rich in good works, to be generous and ready to share." In doing so, they are experiencing verse 19 by laying up future treasure for themselves as a firm foundation for the coming age and thereby taking hold *now*, in the present, of the life that is truly life. In other words, they are, in the deepest sense, living the good life!

Money is a curse whenever we allow it to become the center of our affections, get a stranglehold on us, and choke out the abundant life God intends for us. But when we use it wisely and generously to bless others, we, too, are blessed—both now and in the world to come.

Giving, then, not only brings life change to those

we give to, though that would be reason enough to do it. It also beautifully empowers us and enriches our own lives by refocusing our hearts and investing us in Heaven.

DO GOD'S WARNINGS TO THE RICH APPLY TO US?

Whoever sows sparingly will also reap sparingly, and whoever sows bountifully will also reap bountifully. Each one must give as he has decided in his heart, not reluctantly or under compulsion, for God loves a cheerful giver. 2 CORINTHIANS 9:6-7

You might think that giving is a good idea . . . someday, when you have more money. You may feel like you just don't have extra to give right now. True, compared to Bill Gates, you may not have much. But compared to 98–99 percent of the world, the vast majority of the readers of this booklet have a great deal of money! When it comes to money and possessions, we tend to compare upward, not downward.

In 2017 a family of four in the United States with an annual income of $24,600 was at the US federal poverty level.[6] Yet when I entered that amount at globalrichlist.com, it indicated this income level is in the top 2.09 percent of people worldwide. In 2018 the median household income in the United States was $62,175.[7] That amount lands not just in the top one percent of the world's wealthy but *inside the top one-fifth of one percent.*[8]

Millionaires make up about 4 percent of the US population.[9] It's easy to suppose *those* are the people who qualify as rich. But consider that the quality, variety, and affordability of consumer goods, including technology, available to lower- or middle-class Americans far exceed those available to history's kings and queens!

The truth is, if you and your children are not malnourished or enslaved, and if you can access clean water and shelter, you are comparatively rich on that basis alone.

The next time you're tempted to think, *I don't have enough money to give,* don't compare yourself to the relatively small number of people who have more than you. Compare yourself to the seven billion others who have less—most of them far less.

In other words, Paul's instructions to the rich in 1 Timothy 6:17-19 certainly apply to us.

For those who are rich—including me, and most likely you—the key to avoiding greed, pride, and possessiveness is recognizing God's ownership of everything: "To the LORD your God belong the heavens, even the highest heavens, the earth and everything in it" (Deuteronomy 10:14, NIV).

If we were the ultimate owners of our possessions and money, no one would have the right to tell us what to do with them. Hence, until we truly grasp that God owns everything and that we're merely stewards of his assets, we won't be generous givers.

If those who feel they can't afford to give reduced discretionary spending, lived in smaller homes or apartments, drove older cars, ate out less, or made fewer visits to the coffee shop, a significant amount would be freed up to give. And once we experienced the joy of giving, we would find it more satisfying and of greater enduring value than the nonessentials we might otherwise purchase.

When we understand just how rich we are and truly embrace God's ownership, it's a small step to regularly ask him what he wants us to do with *his* money and possessions.

DOES GOD EXPECT US TO GIVE AWAY *EVERYTHING*?

Command those who are rich in the things of this life not to be proud, but to place their hope, not in such an uncertain thing as riches, but in God, who generously gives us everything for our enjoyment.　1 TIMOTHY 6:17, GNT

PLEASE DON'T MISUNDERSTAND: God doesn't intend for us to give away every possession and every dollar he provides. There is clearly a responsibility to meet the needs of our families *and* a place for enjoying what money can buy, when accompanied by generous giving.

Don't you love that inspired statement that God "generously gives us everything for our enjoyment"? Sure, it should be balanced by the surrounding commands to give generously, but it tells us we don't need to feel guilty for enjoying God's provisions.

In fact, God models the same extravagant generosity he calls us to show others. God owns the universe itself and gives generously even to those who don't know him (Acts 14:17), but he takes special pleasure in giving gifts to his children.

Some of these gifts come to us without cost: a sunrise or the scent of flowers. Trips to places like the Grand Canyon or the Smoky Mountains cost something, but I believe taking such trips to connect with God and our family or friends can fall within the generosity of our gracious God. So can buying good books, enjoying a meal at a favorite restaurant with people we love, or appreciating the companionship of a beloved pet, all of which prompt us to thank God for his kindness. God's generosity abounds. His gifts surround us everywhere we look—and everywhere we don't.

So, no, God doesn't expect his followers to live like monks in a stark cell, never feasting or celebrating or enjoying life. Rather, he is like a parent who puts presents under the Christmas tree and delights in watching his children enjoy what he chose especially for them.

Paul wasn't telling us "Stop enjoying life" in 1

Timothy 6:17, but rather "Start enjoying the good life—the true and abundant life! Take pleasure in all God's gifts to you." He wasn't telling us "Don't care about treasures" but "Enjoy the superior treasures and joys of generosity."

God is the ultimate good parent. He does not cater to our whims or submit to our demands. Yet he is a kind, gracious, and loving Father who cares for our needs and even has a place in his heart for our wants. He gives us surprising, delightful, and frequent treats, while not spoiling us with overindulgence or trouble-free ease.

Our Father doesn't prize our misery or insist we live a life of stoic sacrifice. Rather, the Creator delights in our joy. Who should enjoy God's world more than God's people, who know and love him as their generous Father? His gifts are not merely the best this life has to offer—they are previews of the greater life to come. So we simultaneously feel profound gratitude for what he gives us now and great anticipation for the treasures he promises us in the world to come.

IS MONEY THE ONLY THING WE CAN GIVE?

Truly I tell you, whatever you did for one of the least of these brothers and sisters of mine, you did for me.   MATTHEW 25:40, NIV

THE FOURFOLD EXPRESSION of generosity in 1 Timothy 6:18 ("to do good, to be rich in good works, to be generous and ready to share") doesn't have to be exclusively financial. However, it wouldn't be true to this passage to say, as some have, that it's as much about giving time as it is about giving money.

Paul's terminology relates to money. It's a series of commands specifically to "those who are rich" (1 Timothy 6:17, NIV), not to "those with time on their hands." The person who says, "I can't afford to give to my church, so instead I teach Sunday school" is embracing one important sphere of service while neglecting another. We are to freely give to God and others of our time, energy, skills, wisdom, *and* money and possessions.

Of course, our giving of all these resources need not and will not be perfectly balanced all the time. Sometimes we'll give more time—and with it more energy and wisdom and skills—than money and possessions.

On other occasions, and especially when we live far from the people in need, we will give more money than time.

Personally, I love the picture of Jesus rewarding us someday for things he will have to remind us we did (Matthew 25:40). I also love the thought that when we see people in Heaven, some will thank us for giving to them, including those we never met directly. Certainly God sees, values, and remembers our every act of generosity, even when we don't.

Marjorie Yates says, "I received $1,000 in insurance money after the death of my grandfather. I had decided to give some of it away, and an opportunity arose to send a girl from the juvenile parole program to Young Life's Malibu Club summer camp, where I was volunteering. As a camp counselor, I was assigned a cabin of girls from juvenile parole, all of whom had been sent there by gifts from others. I watched their hearts open to the gospel, and all six made a profession of faith. What a joy it was to see what God did with my gift!"[10]

Thirty-year-old Ana Harris, who has struggled with debilitating Lyme disease for years, writes these eye-opening and biblically resonant words:

> Take heart friends, you may have less energy and health to work with but you can still give what little you can. And in the eyes of Jesus, your feeble expression of gratitude to your caregivers can be more significant than someone else's founding a non-profit. Just give what you have to give. The sick mom heating up canned soup for her family in the microwave may be giving more than the mom who is cooking an all organic meal from scratch. The sick wife who takes three hours to write a simple birthday card in between waves of pain

may be giving more than the healthy wife who organizes a big birthday party. . . . The sick believer who fights to concentrate enough to say a two-sentence prayer for a person in need may be giving more than the healthy ones who are leading Bible studies and starting ministries. The people we love may not always realize this, but we can rest assured that Christ is watching and he knows. He knows our hearts. He knows that what a suffering person has to give looks different than what a healthy person has to give.[11]

As Christ-followers, we are commanded "to be generous and ready to share" (1 Timothy 6:18). We are instructed to give sacrificially, not only of our financial resources, but of our time as well, just as Ana does to the extent she can, and as Marjorie did for the girls at that summer camp. Giving both time and money is vital to embracing the good life God has for us.

HOW DO WE BENEFIT FROM GIVING TO OTHERS?

There is more happiness in giving than in receiving.   ACTS 20:35, GNT

IT'S HUMAN NATURE to imagine that spending on ourselves will make us happiest. But Jesus said, "There is more happiness in giving than in receiving" (Acts 20:35, GNT). You might have heard that verse translated "It is more blessed to give than receive," but the truth is that the Greek word *makarios*, translated here as "blessed," really means "happy" or "happy-making."[12]

Notice what Jesus did *not* say: "Naturally, we're happier when we receive than when we give, but giving is a duty, so grit your teeth, make the sacrifice, and force yourself to give."

In order to experience the good life, it's vital we understand what the Bible clearly reveals: *Money won't make us happy. But giving away money can make us profoundly happy.* When we give out of love for Christ and others, we experience dramatic and lasting returns on the investments we've made—far more than if we'd kept or spent it. Therefore, it's not only receivers who come out ahead when we give—we do too.

In fact, modern research has much to say about the benefits of generosity. In their book *The Paradox of Generosity: Giving We Receive, Grasping We Lose*, sociologists Christian Smith and Hilary Davidson write:

> Giving money, volunteering, being relationally generous, being a generous neighbor and friend, and personally valuing the importance of being a generous person are all significantly, positively correlated with greater personal happiness, physical health, a stronger sense of purpose in life,

avoidance of symptoms of depression, and a greater interest in personal growth.[13]

Still, for many, the thought that giving makes us happier than receiving seems counterintuitive. What could be better than receiving a gift? Don't we love Christmas and our birthdays and receiving packages in the mail?

Sure, receiving a gift is great, and our hearts should be full of praise to God—first and foremost for his Son, but also for thousands of his smaller gifts we seldom think about. We should be profoundly grateful for what others have given us too. But have you ever worked hard to find the perfect gift for someone you love? Or thrown a surprise party for someone or given them tickets to a concert or game? Isn't your joy multiplied by your investment in planning and by the receiver's joy?

I learned of a family sponsoring a child whose son asked them, "Can you help me sell my game system on eBay?" The parents were surprised, since this was one of their son's most prized possessions. They asked him why. "So I can send our child a Christmas present," he replied.

I'm sure the boy was happy when he originally received his game system. I'm also sure that when he gave a Christmas present to a truly needy child across the globe, his happiness was both greater and more lasting.

When we understand how giving touches lives for eternity, stores treasures for us in Heaven, and brings us great happiness here and now, we'll realize there's no greater privilege than to live lives of overflowing love and joyful generosity. Giving is so addictive and fun it eventually becomes instinctive.

Cultivating a habit of generosity may sound like dutiful obedience to the uninitiated. But generous givers know the truth: the practice of generosity ultimately explodes into enduring happiness.

HOW CAN GIVING BECOME AN ADVENTURE?

From one human being he created all races of people and made them live throughout the whole earth. He himself fixed beforehand the exact times and the limits of the places where they would live.   ACTS 17:26, GNT

THE POPULAR EXPRESSION "random acts of kindness" is catchy and good hearted, but as believers in a sovereign God, we should see how he orchestrates our lives, including the people we meet and the needs we encounter. God is not random, nor are the lives he sets before us!

In Acts 17:26 (above), Paul tells how God fixes the exact times and places where people live. Doesn't this suggest he also fixes the times and places we will be on any particular day? Sure, people have free will, but that doesn't mean God can't take into account your free will and mine (and everyone else's) so he can arrange divine appointments.

The next verse tells us the beautiful purpose God has for fixing our exact times and places: "He did this *so that they would look for him, and perhaps find him* as they felt around for him. Yet God is actually not far from any one of us" (Acts 17:27, GNT, emphasis added). Part of our role in divine appointments is helping people look for and find the grace of Jesus. Perhaps having his followers everywhere is part of the way God is not far even from unbelievers. He touches others through us.

I believe that while it's wise to do most of our major giving in a thoughtful, planned way, there's certainly a place for spontaneous giving. But even unanticipated giving is not ultimately random. If you believe in a sovereign God, then being somewhere at a certain time and place when a particular person is also there is not random, but providentially orchestrated by God.

One afternoon, I bought lunch for a stranger at a pizza place (I left my credit card with the cashier while I ate and told her to use it for whoever came in next). As I saw the stranger smile, this thought came to me: *God has me here today, not for a random act of kindness, but to fulfill his ancient plan and purpose. He prepared in advance for me to buy lunch for this man at this place and time.*

I couldn't have put that particular man on my schedule. What I *can* put on my schedule is a giving adventure—a day of giving, where I don't buy anything for myself without giving something to someone else.

Too many of us are bored with our Christian lives because we don't see the daily opportunities for adventure granted us by our sovereign God. The best cure for boredom is one people don't typically consider: giving more time, money, and energy to God's Kingdom work.

One hot summer day I stopped at a store for a Diet Mountain Dew, but when I saw the price, I changed my mind. However, as I often do, I prayed that God would connect me with someone in the store. The few people inside didn't look like they needed anything, so I thought, *Next time*, and left.

Outside, six feet from me, stood a young man who was probably in his early thirties. With long, stringy hair and worn sandals, he looked like he'd been living on the streets. He hadn't been there three minutes earlier when I walked in. I knew he was my answer to prayer.

"Hey, it's a hot day," I said. "Can I get you a bottle of water? Something to eat?"

He looked at me.

Reaching out my hand, I said, "I'm Randy."

He shook my hand. "I'm John."

I was unprepared for what happened next. He looked at me intently and said, "Are you a servant of Yeshua Adonai?"

Recognizing the Hebrew words for Jesus and Lord, or Master, I responded with a stunned "Yes, I am."

He immediately put his hand on my shoulder and prayed for me—as if I were the needy one, which I was that day. His prayer was insightful, biblically resonant, and articulate—in fact, one of the most powerful prayers I've ever heard.

Then I prayed for John. When I finished, I asked him again if I could get something for him in the store. He chose a small water bottle, but I pulled out a large instead (next to the Mountain Dew I was too cheap to buy). "Why don't you pick out something to eat?" I said. He chose some chips, and the total came to $4.50.

When we walked out the door, I tried to engage John further. But it seemed he had someplace to go, so we said good-bye. I went to my car and wept, overcome with the deep sense that I'd met an angel. Hebrews 13:2 says, "Do not forget to show hospitality to strangers, for by so doing some people have shown hospitality to angels without knowing it" (NIV).

If he wasn't an angel, I knew John had been sent by God to pray for me. Who knows—maybe he was Jesus himself, who said whatever we do to the needy we do for him (Matthew 25:40).

After thanking God and regaining my composure, I headed for home, deeply touched. At a stoplight, I looked to my right and saw John thirty feet away, leaning against a building, drinking from his large water bottle. With a big smile, he waved at me in a way that seemed to say, "See you later."

No matter who John really was, I knew without a doubt that I would, in fact, see him later. I suspect we'll sit together at a banquet on the New Earth, and I'll find out who he really is and hear his story. The thought of it thrills me even now.

And I suspect that $4.50 will turn out to be one of the best investments I've ever made.

WHAT LASTING BENEFITS, BEYOND HAPPINESS, WILL WE EXPERIENCE WHEN WE GIVE?

Do not lay up for yourselves treasures on earth, where moth and rust destroy and where thieves break in and steal, but lay up for yourselves treasures in heaven, where neither moth nor rust destroys and where thieves do not break in and steal. For where your treasure is, there your heart will be also.   MATTHEW 6:19-21

OKAY, YOU MIGHT BE thinking, *I understand that giving to others can bring me happiness and even a wonderful sense of adventure to my life. But is there really any benefit beyond that initial good feeling I get when I help someone?*

One of the biggest misconceptions about giving is that the money we part with to help the needy or to spread the gospel just disappears forever. While we hope others will benefit from it, we're quite sure *we* won't. We even buy into the devil's lie that giving will rob us of the good life.

We couldn't be more wrong.

Jesus told his disciples that when they gave money away, their hearts would follow the treasures they were storing in Heaven (Matthew 6:19-21). He also said that at the Resurrection, God would reward them for helping the needy (Luke 14:14). Somehow we're forever connected to what we give and the people we give it to. Martin Luther has been credited with saying, "I have held many things in my hands and I have lost them all. But whatever I have placed in God's hands, that I still possess."

The Bible shows that anything we put in God's hands is an investment in eternity. But that doesn't just mean that *someday* our giving will bring us good. It actually does us good here and now—at the same time it does good for others. That's why the good life is inseparable from generosity.

When it comes to our money and possessions, the old sayings are true: "You can't take it with you" and "You'll never see a hearse pulling a U-Haul." People can put jewelry, prized possessions, and other treasures in their coffins or graves, but these items won't accompany them to the afterlife. Many of the beautiful treasures at the National Museum of Egyptian Civilization had been buried with the pharaohs, with the idea that these belongings would go to the afterlife with them. The souls of the pharaohs are long gone, but their treasures didn't move an inch.

In his words about storing up treasures in Heaven in Matthew 6:19-21, Jesus added a stunning corollary. He essentially said this, in what I call the Treasure Principle: "You can't take it with you, but you *can* send it on ahead."[14]

It's worth noting that Jesus used the same word, *treasures*, for both the things people value on Earth (for instance, money and possessions) and the things we will one day value in Heaven. This doesn't mean the treasures are the same, but it does mean they are parallel.

Just what are these treasures? Jesus is our first and principal eternal treasure. All else pales in comparison to him (Philippians 3:7-11). Heaven is our second treasure—a place where Christ lives and where we are to set our minds (Colossians 3:1-2).

Eternal rewards, our third treasure, seem to center primarily around the positions of service we'll be granted and the friends we will enjoy forever in Heaven because of what we have done with the money God entrusted to us on Earth (Luke 16:9).

Your role in God's Kingdom is not only as a son or daughter of the King but also as an investor, an asset manager, and an eternal beneficiary. Your reward may include the privilege of being a ruler in that Kingdom—a king or queen serving under the King of kings (Daniel 7:18, 27; Luke 19:17).

Who would dare to think such a thing possible—that we creatures of dust can make choices in this life that result in eternal gain? If it were our idea, it would be heresy! But it's not. Jesus said it: when we give to eternal causes the treasures we would otherwise lose, the heavenly treasures we gain will remain ours forever!

HOW IS GIVING AWAY MONEY A WISE INVESTMENT?

Sell your possessions, and give to the needy. Provide yourselves with moneybags that do not grow old, with a treasure in the heavens that does not fail, where no thief approaches and no moth destroys. For where your treasure is, there will your heart be also.   LUKE 12:33-34

THE SCRIPTURAL COMMAND to store up treasures in Heaven proves that giving isn't simply parting with wealth—it's actually transferring wealth to another location, where it can never be lost. In fact, giving to God's Kingdom is the most dependable and profitable investment ever!

We can lose our money to the government or to death, or leave it all to heirs who, in most cases, don't need it or may be tempted to misuse it. Or we can utilize a third alternative: we can give it away now. Giving gives us the greatest control, and also the greatest security, because once we give it away, it can never be lost, wasted, or taken from us.

The moment we give, God is pleased. While we should seek to be wise givers, once we place our money in God's hands, it's up to him to determine how it will make a difference.

Jack Alexander says, "Our giving went to a whole other level when one day I got my first bonus ever. It was $5,000. I organized a dinner at Wendy's with [my wife] Lisa and my two little boys to tell them."

Hearing this news, Lisa responded, "You won't believe what happened today." They had received a letter from a nurse in Sudan who needed to buy a Jeep. The cost of the vehicle? Five thousand dollars!

Jack's initial response was, "Noooooo . . ."

But Lisa said these fateful words: "Will you pray about it?"

"God met me in that prayer, and he showed me two things," Jack says. "First, he showed me . . . the value of probably hundreds of kids who could get inoculations, and people [who] could be helped. I was just overwhelmed with what a great investment it was to give that money away. The second thing I really knew was from the Holy Spirit because I got this overwhelming sense . . . that this was a privilege, that God . . . had chosen us to do it and join his work. And we gave the money away."[15]

Every day of our lives, as we get closer to our deaths, we head away from the treasures we accumulate on Earth. But if we store up our riches in Heaven, every day brings us closer to them. That's why Jesus wants us to let go of much of our stuff and walk with arms wide open toward eternity!

Think of treasures as having mass and, therefore, gravity. Gravity holds things in orbit around that mass. The larger the mass we accumulate—the more treasures we store up on Earth—the greater its gravitational pull on us.

But consider this: the more we invest in eternal interests, the less mass our treasures on Earth have, and therefore the less power they have to hold us in their orbit.

Giving multiplies the mass of our treasures in Heaven. This corresponding increase in Heaven's gravitational pull places us more in orbit around God and his Kingdom and his values. The more we give, the more our center of gravity shifts away from our own temporary earthly kingdoms to Christ's eternal Kingdom.

Giving, then, not only brings life change to the recipients—though that would be reason enough to do it. It also beautifully enriches our own lives by refocusing our hearts and investing us in Heaven. In doing so, giving empowers us to take hold of the good life God intends for us.

IS IT WRONG TO SEEK REWARDS OR TREASURES IN HEAVEN?

Without faith it is impossible to please God, because anyone who comes to him must believe that he exists and that he rewards those who earnestly seek him.   HEBREWS 11:16, NIV

DESPITE THE FACT that 1 Timothy 6:17-19 and numerous other passages clearly teach that God rewards us when we honor and obey him, many sincere but misguided Christians bristle at the idea that we should ever be motivated by rewards.

But before discounting the idea of rewards as a motivator, we need to look at what Scripture says. According to Jesus, God's two most important commandments are to love him and to love others (Matthew 22:36-40). If you told your children there were two things more important than anything else that you were asking them to do, and they did it, would you want to reward them through your praise and gifts of appreciation? Certainly. Does God love his children less than you love yours? Certainly not.

Naturally, reward should never be our *only* motivation. Motivation by gratitude to serve God (Hebrews 12:28) and by our ambition to please him (2 Corinthians 5:9) are also valid. Neither motive conflicts with the motive of reward. The same Bible that calls us to obey out of our love for God as Father and Redeemer (Deuteronomy 7:9; 11:1; 30:20) also calls us to obey out of our fear of him as Creator and Judge (Genesis 18:25; Deuteronomy 28:58-67; Hebrews 10:30-31) and out of our hope in him as Rewarder (Deuteronomy 28:2-9; Hebrews 11:6). Each motivation coexists with and complements the others.

This isn't a matter of mixed motives (some good, some bad). Rather, it's about *multiple* motives—each of them good, and each wired into us by God himself. In concert, these multiple motives reinforce one another and prompt us to gladly serve our Father.

In his kindness and common grace, God

sometimes gives to us even when we don't honor him. But certainly he always grants special rewards to his faithful children. His rewards don't contradict his love; they express it.

God explicitly promises us rewards for giving, including the present rewards of happiness (Acts 20:35) and true abundant life, as well as the eternal rewards of treasures in Heaven (Matthew 6:19-20). What honors Christ is always best for us, and what's best for us always honors Christ.

Many view generosity as virtuous because our giving helps others come out ahead while putting ourselves behind. But that's not how God's economy works. As we've seen in 1 Timothy 6 and Matthew 6, when we give, we are storing up treasure for ourselves. We serve God for his glory, yes, but what is for God's glory is always for our good. There is no conflict whatsoever between serving God and people out of love, and realizing that doing so enriches our own lives.

Of course, God doesn't *have* to reward anyone for anything. He does so because he *wants* to. And regardless of what you and I think about it, that's exactly what he's going to do! So let's learn to be enthusiastically grateful for his extreme generosity to us in making all the promises he does.

"God is not unjust. He will not forget how hard you have worked for him and how you have shown your love to him by caring for other believers, as you still do" (Hebrews 6:10, NLT). God is always watching and will always reward his children, both forever and here and now. "The eyes of the LORD search the whole earth in order to strengthen those whose hearts are fully committed to him" (2 Chronicles 16:9, NLT).

He'll always reward the child who gives to the offering the money she'd saved for a softball mitt.

He'll always reward the teenager who kept himself pure despite temptations.

He'll always reward the man who tenderly cared for his wife with Alzheimer's, the mother who patiently raised the child with cerebral palsy, the child who rejoiced in God despite his disability.

He'll always reward the couple who downsized, selling their large house to live in a small one and give the difference to those in need.

He'll always reward the unskilled who were faithful and the skilled who were meek and servant hearted.

He'll always reward the parents who modeled Christ to their children and the children who followed him despite their parents' mistakes.

He'll always reward those who suffered while trusting him and those who comforted the suffering.

Why? Because that's who he is. It's his nature, his pleasure, and his promise: "The Son of Man is going to come in his Father's glory with his angels, and then he will reward each person according to what they have done" (Matthew 16:27, NIV).

God desires you to want what he has offered— not only the gift of your salvation, but also the abundant rewards and treasures in Heaven he kindly offers to those who serve him faithfully. Your service for him includes giving generously, which is close to his heart and at the very heart of the gospel. He promises that your giving will pay off, both now and forever.

DO WE HAVE TO WAIT FOR HEAVEN TO EXPERIENCE THE GOOD LIFE?

In this way [through generous giving] they will lay up treasure for themselves as a firm foundation for the coming age, so that they may take hold of the life that is truly life. 1 TIMOTHY 6:19, NIV

WHEN WILL WE TAKE hold of that abundant life? Not after we die, but after we give! In fact, after each gift. While the treasures Jesus and Paul spoke of await us in Heaven, attaining the true life happens here and now.

Our investments that result in treasures in Heaven have an expressly stated purpose: "so that" we can take hold of Jesus' gift of abundant life. Of course, that's not the *only* purpose. We give because we love God and people. But 1 Timothy 6:19 also tells us to grab hold of the good life here and now.

We don't need to wonder how to do this. God directly tells us it's by generous giving.

The word meaning "take hold of" indicates a present-tense action that brings results now. In the English Standard Version, it's rendered "seized" in Acts 16:19, 18:17, and 21:30, in contexts where believers are grabbed and dragged away or beaten. This aggressive word implies that we must vigorously, tenaciously clutch this life. If we don't, it will slip away.

I believe we can take hold of only one kind of life at a time. In order to take hold of the life that is truly life, we must say no to a life of pride, self-deification, sex-obsession, and money-love. We must say no to the pathetic "life" spent craving Facebook and Instagram likes and viewing the world through the lens of a selfie. We must reject what our world calls the good life and embrace what God tells us is *the* good life.

We simply cannot say yes to God's promises of overflowing abundant life without simultaneously and consciously saying no to the false claims of the one whom Jesus called "a liar and the father of lies" (John 8:44). Giving helps us do exactly that.

HOW CAN WE GIVE GENEROUSLY WITHOUT WORRYING?

Do not be anxious about your life, what you will eat or what you will drink, nor about your body, what you will put on. Is not life more than food, and the body more than clothing? Look at the birds of the air: they neither sow nor reap nor gather into barns, and yet your heavenly Father feeds them. Are you not of more value than they? MATTHEW 6:25-26

MAYBE YOU ARE on board with what you've read so far, yet you still think, *If I give generously, I'll worry about how to get the money to replace what I've given.* But Jesus teaches that generous giving isn't a cause for insecurity and worry. It's a cure for it.

Immediately after he commands us not to store up treasures on Earth but to store them in Heaven (Matthew 6:19-21), Jesus says we are to adopt the right perspective (verses 22-23) and serve the right master—God, not money (verse 24).

Our Lord follows this statement by saying three times, "Do not worry" (Matthew 6:25, 31, 34, NIV). Those who invest in the right treasury, adopt the right perspective, and serve the right master have nothing to worry about. In contrast, those who invest in the wrong treasury (Earth, not Heaven), adopt the wrong perspective (the temporal, not the eternal), and serve the wrong master (money, not God) have every reason to worry.

After Jesus tells us not to worry about life's necessities—specifically food, drink, and clothes—he says, "But seek first the kingdom of God and his righteousness, and all these things will be added to you" (Matthew 6:33). According to our Lord, giving isn't the problem that will leave us short of material provision. In fact, it's part of the solution to our material needs, since God promises to provide for givers, just as he did in Old Testament times (Malachi 3:8-11). Jesus promises the same (Luke 6:38). When we give away our treasures, we are seeking God's Kingdom first. This is the very thing Jesus says fulfills the condition for his promise to provide the material goods we need.

Gerard and Geraldine Low of Singapore believe

that God wants us to test his promises to provide, and trust him to show his greatness and sufficiency. Every year the Lows pray and decide how much they are going to give. But almost without fail, crises arise, bringing financial instability to the point that they have wondered if they could—or should—give at the level they've determined.

Still, they've stuck to their commitment, even when it has meant dipping into their savings. "We're accountants by training," Gerard says, "so we started a spreadsheet of what we've promised to give to God. Each time we almost run out of money to give to God, God restores our lost income and provides the means for us to continue giving."[16] They are taking God at his word when he invites us to test him in this area. "If you don't let go, you're not giving Him a test," Geraldine says.[17]

Like the Lows and countless others, my wife, Nanci, and I have been amazed and thankful to see God come through again and again. The more you experience this, the greater your joy and delight and trust in God. For thirty years, Nanci and I have had the privilege of giving away all our book royalties to God's Kingdom work. On occasion, people ask if I realize what we could have done with all the money from the sale of more than eleven million books. The answer is easy: "Nothing that would bring us nearly as much joy!"

I'm certainly not saying that God must always give back to us exactly what we give up, or ten or a hundred times more, in some kind of karma-like transaction or misapplication of Mark 10:30. Sometimes he gives us joy or patience or endurance as we make real sacrifices for him—and such intangible gifts are absolutely priceless.

But when more material provision does come back, whatever you do, don't hold it tightly. God has told us precisely why he provides for us so abundantly: "You will be made rich in every way so that you can be generous in every way" (2 Corinthians 9:11, CEB). The verse continues, "Such generosity produces thanksgiving to God."

Keep joyfully giving back to God by meeting the physical and spiritual needs of others. Don't wait for your treasures to follow your heart; instead, give your treasures freely, then watch your heart follow them to what will matter when this life is done.

This is the good life, the adventure of trusting

God and seeing him work in us and through us and around us. This is the abundant life of excitement and happiness, to be followed by the unending pleasures of eternal life with God and his people in a renewed and vastly improved universe.

HOW DO I TEACH MY CHILDREN TO BE GENEROUS?

Train up a child in the way he should go, and when he is old he will not depart from it.   PROVERBS 22:6, NKJV

MOST CHRISTIAN PARENTS who unthinkingly raise their children to love money don't set out with that goal in mind. In fact, they would probably say that more than anything else, they want their children to walk with God (not wander from the faith) and be happy (not pierce themselves with many griefs). But as 1 Timothy 6:9-10 makes clear, as does life experience, children raised in materialism are prime candidates to wander from God.

Children with access to larger amounts of money will face larger and more frequent temptations. Just as greater mass exerts stronger gravitational pull, the more money and possessions our children have, the more strongly they will be pulled toward those possessions, and the more tightly children will be held in their orbit. Though neither they nor their parents likely desire it, those with access to more money find it easier to trust money rather than God.

In contrast, if parents say no to both their own and their children's momentary wants, and say yes to giving more radically, it is more likely that they and their children will be drawn to God, the source of happiness. By not purchasing expensive electronics or the latest video games, we may free our children to read and play outside and interact face-to-face with others. Ultimately, they will be healthier and happier for it.

Of course, the most influential lesson in living simply and giving generously is the way we live. Like everything else in the home, stewardship and generosity are caught as much as taught. Children will do what we do more often than they will do what we say. Through example, we can teach our children to avoid greed, to control spending, and to give generously.

With deliberate and sustained effort, and through the power of God at work in us and our children, we can model a different path—a path that is the good life. Even in a world under the Curse, this path is infused with an eternal perspective and a supernatural happiness.

WHAT ARE YOU WAITING FOR?

Teach us to number our days that we may get a heart of wisdom.   PSALM 90:12

SINCE SATAN IS a chronic liar and is bent on robbing us of the good life in Jesus, it's likely that the moment you put down this booklet, you'll be tempted to forget how God might have prompted you as you read. Jesus tells us to be generous and eager to share right now, in the present. If you wait until you have no doubts or worries, you'll probably never take that next step. But if you do take that step by faith, you will find it exhilarating. Ultimately, giving may be the healthiest and most joy-saturated addiction you'll ever experience.

Don't let the devil whisper rationalizations to keep you from a transformed life. Don't let him convince you that it's better to hold tight to what you have. And don't let him tempt you to think, *Sure, someday when I make a lot more money, then I'll start giving.* If you buy into that, it will simply never happen.

While our adversary argues that giving will rob us of the good life, Jesus tells us the truth: giving generates the good life. Now the only question is, whom will we believe?

Jesus makes it clear that the abundant life consists not in material abundance but in the life-giving spiritual abundance found only in him. Eternal and abundant life begins in this world when we come to Jesus, the ultimate giver, and continues as we become more like him.

The gospel itself centers on the single greatest act of giving in the history of the universe: "You know the grace of our Lord Jesus Christ, that though he was rich, yet for your sake he became poor, so that you through his poverty might become rich" (2 Corinthians 8:9, NIV).

God says we can experience the authentic

abundant life in Christ by being generous and eager to share. Generosity simultaneously stores up eternal treasures in Heaven, gives vital help to the needy, and front-loads eternal joy into our present lives.

It's critical that you take hold of the good life *now* and use the limited window of time God has entrusted to you to invest in eternity. After you leave this world, you will never have another chance to move the hand of God through prayer. Or heal a hurting soul. Or share Christ with someone who can be saved from Hell. Or care for the sick. Or serve a meal to the starving. Or comfort the dying. Or rescue the unborn. Or translate the Scriptures into someone's heart language. Or bring the gospel to an unreached people group. Or open your home. Or share your clothes and food with those in need.

Death puts our signature on our life's portrait. The paint dries. The portrait is permanently finished. No future renovation is possible. When the final buzzer sounds, no more points can be scored, and the outcome is permanent. This is your opportunity, right here and now, to grab hold of the good life and experience all that God has for you!

I can't tell you exactly what it will look like for

you to embrace the abundant life Jesus offers you. I don't know what you've read in this booklet that the Holy Spirit might use to move these truths from theory to reality. But I can tell you with absolute certainty that committing to live the generous life to God's glory will both please and honor him *and* at the same time infuse you with Christ-centered happiness. Someday, almost certainly in this life but for sure in the next one, you will realize it was on the short list of most important decisions you ever made.

Perhaps this will require making some lifestyle changes to loosen the grip of material things and free up more money to invest in God's Kingdom. Maybe God is calling you to downsize your home, drive an older car, sell some jewelry, give away a portion of your savings, forgo an expensive vacation, or skip some lattes or dinners out so you can find more to give away. Perhaps you'll be led to invest your time and money in serving at a local ministry and reaching out to needy people in your city and neighborhood. Maybe you'll plan some giving adventures where you pay for people's groceries or meals and discover that what some call random acts of kindness are actually divine appointments.

I can assure you that once you experience the good life, the abundant life, the generous life, you will never want to settle for less. Life will never be the same—nor will you want it to be!

ABOUT THE AUTHOR

RANDY ALCORN is an author and the founder and director of Eternal Perspective Ministries (EPM), a nonprofit organization dedicated to teaching principles of God's Word and assisting the church in ministering to unreached, unfed, unborn, uneducated, unreconciled, and unsupported people around the world. His ministry focus is communicating the strategic importance of using our earthly time, money, possessions, and opportunities to invest in need-meeting ministries that count for eternity.

Before starting EPM in 1990, Randy served as a pastor for fourteen years. He has a bachelor of theology and a master of arts in biblical studies from Multnomah University and an honorary doctorate from Western Seminary in Portland, Oregon.

A *New York Times* bestselling author, Randy has written more than fifty books, including *Heaven*, *The Treasure Principle*, and the award-winning novel *Safely Home*. Over eleven million copies of his books have been sold, and his titles have been translated into more than seventy languages. All royalties from his books are given to the works of Christian ministries, including world missions and organizations that care for the poor.

Randy resides in Gresham, Oregon, with his wife, Nanci. They have two married daughters and are the proud grandparents of five grandsons.

ENDNOTES

1. Karen S. Schneider and Bob Meadows, "Owen Wilson: What Happened?" *People*, September 10, 2007, https://people.com/archive/cover-story-owen-wilson-what-happened-vol-68-no-11/.

2. Kim Teller, letter to the editor, *People*, December 10, 2007, https://people.com/archive/mailbag-vol-68-no-24/.

3. Charles R. Swindoll, *Strengthening Your Grip: How to Be Grounded in a Chaotic World* (Brentwood, TN: Worthy Books, 2015), 88.

4. For more information about Celebration of Generosity events, see https://generousgiving.org/celebrations.

5. "Alan and Nathan Barnhart," Vimeo video, 19:33, Generous Giving, https://generousgiving.org/media/videos/alan-nathan-barnhart.

6. Lindsay Wissman, "2017 Federal Poverty Level Guidelines," PeopleKeep, February 7, 2017, https://www.peoplekeep.com/blog/2017-federal-poverty-level-guidelines.

7. "June 2018 Median Household Income," Seeking Alpha,

August 1, 2018, https://seekingalpha.com/article
/4193310-june-2018-median-household-income.

8. Globalrichlist.com also allows you to calculate your relative wealth by entering the equity in your home and the total value of all your possessions and investments.

9. Michael Douglass, "Here's How Many American Millionaires There Are," Motley Fool, January 23, 2017, https://www.fool.com/retirement/iras/2017/01/23/heres -how-many-american-millionaires-there-are.aspx.

10. Facebook comment in reply to my post requesting giving stories.

11. Ana Harris, "When You Don't Have Much to Offer," Ana Harris Writes (blog), January 10, 2018, http:// anaharriswrites.com/when-you-dont-have-much-to-offer/.

12. Randy Alcorn, *Happiness* (Carol Stream, IL: Tyndale, 2015), 217–24.

13. Christian Smith and Hilary Davidson, *The Paradox of Generosity: Giving We Receive, Grasping We Lose* (New York: Oxford University Press, 2014), 44.

14. Randy Alcorn, *The Treasure Principle*, rev. ed. (Colorado Springs: Multnomah, 2017).

15. "Jack and Lisa Alexander: 2015 Celebration of Generosity," Vimeo video, 20:25, Generous Giving, https://generousgiving.org/media/videos/jack-lisa -alexander.

16. Cameron Doolittle, "Three Lessons on Giving from Gerard and Geraldine Low," Generosity Path, December 12, 2016, http://www.generositypath.org/morestories/ low?rq-Low.

17. Ibid.

HELPING CHILDREN FALL IN LOVE WITH JESUS SO THEY CAN FALL IN LOVE WITH THE WORLD.

Children all over the world have the same needs: to be known, loved, cared for, and protected.

For some children, having these needs met is a delightful reality. But for many others, it is almost impossible to experience, because extreme poverty tells them they don't matter. Although poverty is often measured materially, it spills out emotionally and spiritually as well.

Jesus had compassion on the poor. When your children love Jesus and see the world through His eyes, compassion is a God-inspired response to need. Tyndale and Compassion International come together to create resources to help children fall in love with Jesus so they can follow His example to love others—especially those who live in poverty.

YOUR LOVE FOR ONE ANOTHER WILL PROVE TO THE WORLD THAT YOU ARE MY DISCIPLES. —JOHN 13:35

Compassion
Release children from poverty

WWW.EVERYONENEEDSCOMPASSION.COM   CP1473